SOFT ANIMALS

BRIAN RIGG

STEEL TOE BOOKS
est. 2003
WINSTON-SALEM, NC

All Rights Reserved

Printed in the United States of America

First Edition
1 2 3 4 5 6 7 8 9

Selections of up to two pages may be reproduced without permissions. To reproduce more than two pages of any one portion of this book write to Steel Toe Books.

Cover Art by Kim Atlin

Copyright ©2021 by Brian Rigg

ISBN 978-1-949540-30-7

Steel Toe Books
steeltoebooks.com

SOFT ANIMALS

Contents

Land's End

An Ink Spot, Your Red Dress, the Running Gutter	8
April 14, 1998	9
Hammers & Tongues	10
Propaganda	11
The Archaeology of Beds	12
To Bruise the Rusted Sky	13
The Treachery of All This	14
Found Pieces	15
Three Days in September	16

Soft Animals

[I remember you in that wild]	18
[Then the surprise of his single eye]	19
[We steal each other's lives here]	20
[Together we wrote a whole body]	21
[I begin, like you, from a resonant echo]	22
[In the eventide you become something older]	23
[Every now and again you become the full kingdom of sorrows]	24
[As the morning mists over the lake]	25
[There is an animal agenda here]	26
[As a dog I see you, holding]	27

This Is You Boy!

Ode to Lady M	30
Triptych for New Orleans	32
At Madame Isabelle's House	32
On Bourbon Street	33
In Jackson Square	34
Before Ballroom	35
Acknowledgments	36
About the Author	37

for Sarah de Vries

This was the land's end: the last fingers, knuckled and rheumatic,
Cramped on nothing. Black
Admonitory cliffs, and the sea exploding
With no bottom, or anything on the other side of it,
Whitened by the faces of the drowned.

-From Sylvia Plath's "Finisterre."

Land's End

An Ink Spot, Your Red Dress, the Running Gutter

That day she slept with the icicles,
her hands splayed wide apart in the open snow.
Coming up after almost drowning,
the repeated wet slaps of her dark hair
against the corrugated zinc, she walks
cautiously through the logged cabin door.

From there she could hear
the strangled
choking of this morning,
the rope anchored to her breath.

She is making muffled
sounds so soft like snowflakes
falling on the windowsill.

After coming inside, drenched,
she drifts over to the cutting board,
her butchered meat laid out upon it.

April 14, 1998

At the edge of Crow Trail
she watches the light blink red as a cyclopean eye.
Her shaking hands caress the crinkle in her dress,
palms like faces shorn jagged and hollowed out.

She loses days here in the muted corridors,
stumbles up Hastings and wanders through a wilderness
of dew soaked pavement
down empty, windblown streets.

She lost more than days here, peering
over the heads of dandelions, the wild thistles
clawing at her scratched knees,
her lungs rushing into so much air.

Hammers & Tongues

Today, she saw no distinction between blood and sex.
Legs splayed, lifeless – the bones spoke of
tattoos etched with nails, hammers, and tongues.

No distinction in this long parade of skin and head,
their idle boredom waiting to spring.

She knew every man on this side of the city was made of charcoal
and sinew, their donkey masks indifferent
to experiments in forced submission.

Tomorrow they will build hollow pipes, the sparks licking
that old industrial skin,
In that alley, for three days of pure hot stench and looming sun,
she is just inside, just out of reach, beyond something like grace.

Propaganda

Her memories are now quick breaths of reckless flame
riding the diesel exhaust of progress on the wasted earth.
She is astride the bony tooth of industry, gestating in the fertile
wombs of revolution and cold fusion.

Years from now she will be studied.

For now, she sits Shiva. She mourns for monsoon smudged coastlines,
heavy rains washing away the tenuous deposits of her so-called life

She is reborn riding a mirrored horse,
her skin the consistency of a thousand lenses.
Her name will be Propaganda.

The Archaeology of Beds

When the girls started to disappear, the leaves held their sway
for a while. The sun swung black as a crescent lid
and closed itself away.
The sky fell down.

After they went astray, she became wary of sound,
the breathing of every empty moment,
every morning the archaeology of her bed,
artefacts of choked linens
on battered pillows, where she found
those old dry stains, again.

The doors threatened to close in.
Short distances became ominous, and the days humbled down,
preparing themselves for the long stretch of shadow into night.

To Bruise the Rusted Sky

One night, after running, she fell down and listened to the sound of
earthworms struggling in the wet soil, a john's retreating steps.
She yearned then for rooftops.

She bruised the rusted sky with outstretched arms and
tried again for a treacherous foot hold on soft earth, strained
to hear the telltales of crickets yearning in the nearby bush.

She was somehow sure he would find her,
pry open her eyes like lotuses in the night's sky,
then drown the half-moon within them.

She noticed up here the air was as thin as paper.
Her hopes ran varicose.
Sullen moths flew from her throat.

The Treachery of All This

The lure of the next fix, the treachery of all this,
she is still plummeting, still concerned for the stains
on her skirt, and careful not to trigger the thunder of sirens.

Her voice is a husky drawl.
When she bends into the car window, she is careful
not to breathe in the last days of his dying youth,
ready to become a doe and spring,
to cover her head with a shawl
and jack-knife into darkness
at the first witness of sin.

Oh give her blizzards and opening flowers
not these aching limbs and nothing but
the endless days of white December.

Found Pieces

She left pieces of her body here, like leaves
along the creek, its waters running sepia
in the June dusk.

Her limbs are discarded Barbies
washed up along the shore
with the ebb and push of waves.
Careless caress of deadwood and stone,
her left eye is somewhere in a crow's nest.

They found pieces of her that day
after the constant sifting through mud,
the moist afternoon hanging on the skin of bark
and the well-trained dogs.
No refuge in the shade,
there was dirt everywhere,
the cloying stench of old pig shit on the farm.

A ghost, she watches the others now,
down on their hands and knees wondering
what happened to the other women, and how much time
did they have to keep fighting for air, right here?

Three Days in September

Three days in September, you spent with the rats;
clutching your stomach, you couldn't move.

You felt safe among the needles and condoms,
your rolled up leg warmers an adequate pillow.
For a second you realized you had only one shoe.

But the retching drew you back to
all you knew of this little world; the broken stairs,
and cracked tiles, the rusted-brown toilet
where you threw up in.

Soft Animals

I

I remember you in that wild,
early spring, when
the trilliums shone anew,
but you hungered for more—
"Lilacs bloom in a month or two."

After the rain, you crept in
to my lungs by way of moonshine
through my two front teeth.
You muted my steps,
sentenced my breath,
and no amount of "ahchoo"
will get you out.

II

The surprise of your single eye,
a lone Susan black as despair;
the hollow sound of cows belling
as they drink at the water's edge;

they join the loon's lonely call
on the hot waves of noon,
they echo in the cave of my black, black heart,
not shorn out, but shackled in.

You posed as a bloody flower, but were really
the spider under it. You arose,
and that is when I chose to spring.

III

We steal each other's lives here,
play a circle game of horrors
by the crackling wood, make
an Ouroboros of leeches.
We spent our afternoons floating down

the drowning horse,
its red-mane's glare guarding a sentinel lake.
Each day breaks its oar against
the constant waves of my face.

In return, by the lavender bush,
I steal your kiss on Larose Bay Road,
feel the fragrant rush of wind

through the leaves and the woods.
There we spoke a half dead tongue,
our words amputated at the throat.

IV

And together we wrote a whole body,
one colony unto our own.
Gaoler you have become, and I the goal.
Tell me the end of this story, tell it wrong,
for I have become an obstacle on my own road
that refuses to be done
and only in twilight were you
bone white and marble glowing among
the stones, fixed in thought.
Here I am in good company with so many silences
and only the sound of rain
gently kissing the leaves.

V

I began, like you, from a resonant echo,
my first breath, a shiver of leaves rustling
my brown body, the penumbra of creation.
I am a new word, born yearning
to begin a conversation
with acorn and sapling, the brown tinged fern,
the soft, silence bed of green moss
rolling past the fire pit
nestled in the deep shoulder
of turtle's point.

VI

In the eventide you become something older,

a throwback alpha, your scent honed to my
secret museum of weaknesses and hollow bones.

That night we burned the dried leaves, branches,
pine cones, the dead limbs of other trees,
the daily mass of indignities.

In the crook of moss, on a soft bed
built on needles of prickly pine,
we listened to Cohen,
sipped on old coffee, and late red wine.

VII

Every now and again you become
the full kingdom of sorrows, restored glory unborn.

At the beginning of that unravelled story,
like the sudden cruel weather,
the sun setting in a violet hue,
you reveal your always,
but this is you, boy,
my thinking the world is the size of you,
yet nowhere in the delicate spin.

Carelessly perched on the edge of a string,
you are the most beautiful singing
of the dirtiest thing.
Suddenly, you are some variety of gone,
a genetic dead end left adrift.

VIII

As the morning mists over the lake,
you send out tendrils.
Slowly, you become something medieval,
your scent honed to my secret
museum of soft buttons and old bones.

By the afternoon, we posted on fences of "I'm sorry,"
laid lines of "I didn't mean to hurt you."
On the sun speckled path,
I allowed a border crossing.

Your soft blowing against
my skin erased in this one act of "there are
no safe words" and "I take it all back."

IX

There is an animal agenda here:
the long gaze into my eyes,
how before me you change into a priest of dogs,
vicious in your loyalty.

Your russet howls reach up into the listening trees.
In the dark, I am caught.
Your ghostly green lights are consumed
by promises of things better left buried
under brown grass and snow.

And so, you do not want this picture taken,
checking behind you for signs of my pursuit.

X

As a dog I see you, holding
the bone of the forest,
the mud and marsh,
your fleeting throne.

Gaping nose feasting on
every winded pheromone;
a green roar;
the heat of midday sun;
your panting breath like clouds—
are every permutation of "yes."

This Is You Boy!

Ode to Lady M
-for Colson

In her hidden garden, she
would sew and sew and sew,
her supple skin a deep furrow.
The hot flow of blood
down a sore-ridden back,
the children of this village and that
would cry and cry their sorrow.

To the dusty bowls of windy lanes
like some dreadful kind of fate:
a noosed neck, a gathered crowd,
red poppies turned to paste,
the devils roar cruel and loud
their thirsty hate to slake.

Even among chameleon boys
playing at wise and strong,
she knew it'd take much more to break
than just another song.

Become then a legend of your kind,
dispatching the nastier strains
of blood with murderous pains.
Yet save some mercy for those
of colonized mind: the Uncle Toms,
the step n' fetch,
and them as toe the line.

Righteous black Lady Macbeth,
your welcome crime not just on hands,
but a stain down the front of your dress.
You will ride the rail and walk
the road until the end of time.

Winston Clairfeld III, 5th Operator, Tennessee to Indiana route. Excerpt from Poems Underground.

Triptych for New Orleans

I At Madame Isabelle's House

Small and unsmiling
her old beauty worked then
betrayed by the sun sneaking
into the courtyard where she
lies cool in the cool shade.

Her skin has grown hard like
the alone turtle eyeing the carp,
a glint of circling gold
fire in the grey rock pool.

II On Bourbon Street

Unwashed are these white walls crumbling
into grey dust, his black skin
the hot white of this one day.

His black head is bowed stone,
brought low between crouched legs:
a dirt statue gathering rust
where iron shatters bone.

III In Jackson Square

We were rendered moot,
we were the root cause, inconsequential
in agony, and over our heads
they lowered a noose.

But we should've known better,
and as long as we got
love and forgiveness
in our hearts,
we won't kill you –
but cut you loose.

Before Ballroom
-for Gia Love

Who was I before Ballroom?
The flop to the ground, the drum,
the pound of the bass, the beating
of my flesh and the demands of that
sweaty, sweet sound.

I am the cis and the boom, the vapors
and the swoon, the promise
of the come soon.

Where was I before Ballroom?
At the edge of my youth,
the end of a rage
tightly coiled and waiting
to unfurl.

Girl, you know the wanting
so bad out of this cage,
for the drop kick and fall back
to death and rebirth of an age,
a body in exquisite disarray
and limbs splayed.

I know my people will catch me
when I fall.
For this is not a suicide
we always attempt,
we respond to the call.

What was I before Ballroom?
A perfect story inside my head,
one where I'm not already dead.
The dread of daddy knowing,
the street and the cred.

Acknowledgements

Several poems from *Land's End* first appeared under the title "The Sarah Diaries" in *Emerge: Lambda Fellows Anthology*, 2016. "Ode to Lady M" has previously appeared under the title "The Ballad of Lady" in *The Hawaii Review*, Issue 91, February 2021. "Before Ballroom" has previously appeared in *The A3 Review*, Issue #9, October 2018.

I'd like to thank the Toronto Arts Council, The Ontario Arts Council and The Canada Council for the Arts for their continued financial support of my writing and creative development.

My deepest gratitude to Alan Wright, for sharing his life and love of poetry with me. Also, for scouring my work like the ever-watchful eye of Sauron.

Unfathomable gratitude to my mother, Carmen Louise Rigg, for birthing, caring, and loving me to this moment.

I'd also like to thank Maggie de Vries for researching and writing *Missing Sarah: A Memoir of Loss*.

I am proud to call Toronto, Canada my home and recognize that I live on traditional Indigenous territories of many nations. These territories include the Mississaugas of the Credit, the Anishnabeg, the Chippewa, the Haudenosaunee and the Wendat peoples and is now the home to many diverse First Nations, Inuit and Metis peoples. I also acknowledge that Toronto is covered by Treaty 13 signed with the Mississaugas of the Credit, and the Williams Treaties signed with multiple Mississauga and Chippewa bands. I acknowledge that there are 46 treaties and other agreements that cover the territory now called Ontario. I am thankful to the First Nations, Metis and Inuit people who have cared for these territories since time immemorial and who continue to contribute to the strength of Ontario and to all communities across the province.

Acknowledging traditional Indigenous territories is one way to recognize contemporary and historical Indigenous presence and land rights. It is a small step towards dismantling the continued impacts of colonialism and undoing Indigenous erasure in our everyday lives.

About the Author

Brian Rigg's poems has been recently published in *The Hawaii Review, Genre: Urban Arts: House Vol.2*, and *A3 Review*. His work has been anthologised in *Ma'ka: Diasporic Juks: Contemporary Writing by Queers of African Descent* and *Seminal: The Anthology of Canada's Gay Male Poets*. He is the author of a previous volume of poetry, *A False Paradise* (ECW Press, 2001). He has been the recipient of grants from the Toronto Arts Council, The Ontario Arts Council and the Canada Council for the Arts. He is a proud 2016 LAMBDA Fellow.

www.ingramcontent.com/pod-product-compliance
Lightning Source LLC
Chambersburg PA
CBHW051705040426
42446CB00009B/1307